What More Can I Do?

David L. Fleming SJ

An Ignatian Retreat
For People Somewhere on the Way

Review for Religious
3601 Lindell Boulevard
St. Louis, Missouri 63108

ISBN 0-924768-14-2

Dedication

For the women and men and my fellow Jesuits,
with whom I was privileged to share
these reflections for prayer.

—Loyola, Spain, August 2006

"We want you to serve us."

–St. Ignatius's vision at La Storta

Contents

Prayer at the Beginning of the Retreat

Lord Jesus,
help us to seek you in all things
and to discover your grace
in the ordinariness of our lives.
Grant us the openness and generosity
to strengthen your church on earth.
May we be your faithful companions,
and rejoice in your presence among us.
We ask this in your name
Our Lord and Savior. Amen.

Foreword
Beginning the Retreat

As we begin the retreat, I have a combination of thoughts that I would like to share with you. I intend that all these thoughts lead to a single focus for our retreat prayer.

The focus is the grace prayed for in the final exercises of the Exercises book, "The Contemplation on the Love of God." In abbreviated form, the grace may be stated: "in all things to love and to serve"—in Ignatius's Spanish, "*en todo amar y servir.*"

I want for us to explore and pray about what it means for us "to serve." Too often I believe that we think of service in a rather restricted way of "getting things done," "a job accomplished." It seems to me that if we use a reflective approach to the gospels, we begin to see how expansive the notion of "to serve" is as Jesus would indicate to us. And so our retreat will be exploring through gospel contemplations all the richness involved in the experience of "to serve." Our prayer will always center on the theme "in all things to love and to serve."

Another thought strikes me about our retreat. I believe that in each retreat, we are asking ourselves, at least implicitly, "what more?" What more can I, should I, be doing for Christ? What more is God asking of me? The same question is before us till the end of our lives. As I interact with the Jesuits in our own province infirmary, I am always edified by their willingness, even eagerness, to try to make sense of their own response to that question "what more?" at this time of their declining years. The "more" is always in terms of loving service.

So "what more?" is the question that also permeates every prayer period of our retreat. What more is God inviting me to, what more is God asking, what more can I give, what more do I want to give?

I identify this retreat as an Ignatian retreat for people somewhere on the way. It is an Ignatian retreat because it has movement and direction. True, in using a book like this for your retreat, it will not have for many of you the help of a director who listens to how you have prayed for a grace and how God has been answering your prayer in such a way as to better point the direction of the next day's prayer. In presenting these retreat conferences, I can only more generally point the direction of each day's prayer. But the direction for me and for you is always caught up in that question, "what more?" Our movement is in terms of responding to God's "what more?" asked of us.

At the same time I am presuming that all of us in this retreat are "somewhere on the way." We are not newcomers to Ignatian spirituality. We all have some previous experience of Ignatian retreats, perhaps even an experience of the full Spiritual Exercises in one of its forms. We all are "somewhere on the way." Being somewhere on the way, in this retreat we are centering our prayer about how we are serving God and others. What more is God asking of us now?

There is a long tradition that has associated a prayer titled "A Prayer for Generosity" with Ignatius Loyola. The prayer reads:

> Lord, teach me to be generous.
> Teach me to serve you as you deserve.
> To give, and not to count the cost.
> To fight, and not to heed the wounds.
> To toil, and not to see for rest.
> To labor, and not to ask for reward,
> Save that of knowing that I am doing your will.

The spirit of the prayer is Ignatian. I want this prayer to permeate the time that we have for this retreat. The first two lines of this prayer will become a mantra that I will repeat at the end of each of our points period. And I hope that it will become the prayer mantra permeating the free time of your day.

There is no doubt that Ignatian spirituality is an apostolic spirituality. Our relationship with God develops through our loving service. It makes sense that we should pray that the Lord will teach us how to serve. Ignatian retreats are known for their movement or dynamic. Our movement in this retreat will be grounded in our seeking to have the Lord teach us how we are to grow in our service. The Ignatian goal of the Spiritual Exercises might be said to be summed up in the phrase "*en todo amar y servir,*" "in all things to love and to serve." In this retreat adaptation, we pray that we might be empowered to serve in all the ways that God's grace leads us. As Ignatius emphasizes throughout the Exercises, " to serve" flows from "to love." God desires our loving service.

In our retreat, then, we want to be attentive to the ways that Jesus calls us to serve. The prayer mantra expresses our retreat direction: "Lord, teach us to be generous. Teach us to serve you as you deserve."

I suggest, then, that in our prayer as we begin this retreat might be this "prayer for generosity." I would encourage us to use Ignatius's second method of prayer suggested at the end of the Exercises book. We can take individual words or phrases and let them resonate inside our being, with all their meaning and affect for us. If one word or phrase holds us, let us stay with it for however long God is holding us close. At the end of our prayer time, let us pray the entire prayer through. And if we want, then we will close our prayer time with an Our Father.

9

Beginning the Retreat

Use the Second Method of Prayer as described by St Ignatius in the Spiritual Exercises [252] – [257]

We can understand the second method of praying in the following way. We use the following Prayer for Generosity as our example. Our position during such prayer can be kneeling or sitting, whichever seems to be more conducive to praying and better fitted to our own devotion. We take care to keep our attention focused in the method of praying by taking advantage of a help like keeping our eyes closed or fixing our gaze upon some one place or horizon or object of devotion. As we begin our prayer, we say "Lord, teach" and we let this word remain within us for so long a time as we find meaning, comparisons, relish, and consolations coming from our reflections on the word. We act in a similar way with every word or phrase of the Generosity Prayer.

A Prayer for Generosity

Lord, teach me to be generous.
Teach me to serve you as you deserve.
To give, and not to count the cost.
To fight, and not to heed the wounds.
To toil, and not to see for rest.
To labor, and not to ask for reward,
Save that of knowing that I am doing your will.

What More Can I Do?

Prayer at the Beginning of the Retreat

Lord Jesus,
help us to seek you in all things
and to discover your grace
in the ordinariness of our lives.
Grant us the openness and generosity
to strengthen your church on earth.
May we be your faithful companions,
and rejoice in your presence among us.
We ask this in your name
Our Lord and Savior. Amen.

11

To Love: A Context of God Speaking

Prayer

God of all good gifts, be generous to us as we
begin this retreat. Let us experience your presence,
your power, and your grace. Help us to know your
goodness in the many ways that you have gifted
us. Draw us close to you so that we can listen even
to the most whispered language of your love.
Move us to respond to your calls with all our heart.
We make our prayer in Jesus' name. Amen.

One
To Love:
A Context of God Speaking

Pope Benedict XVI wrote his first encyclical on the love of God. He drew upon the writings of the evangelist John and so used the title "Deus Caritas Est." Many say that the first encyclical of a pope sets the direction and tone for the whole papacy. Benedict has presented an all-encompassing vision for human life lived with a depth of meaning and has given us all hope as he gives us this context for his papacy.

On this first full day of the retreat I too would like to provide a context for our prayer and reflections. I want to use the context of love from St. Ignatius. I will be drawing upon two structural exercises from St. Ignatius's *Spiritual Exercises*. The first exercise that I will use is the last exercise of the Ignatian 30-day retreat. It is an exercise titled "The Contemplation on the Love of God."

In the text, the grace expressed in the second prelude speaking out what we desire and pray for is that of an intimate knowledge of all the goods which God lovingly shares with us so that filled with gratitude we may be able "in all things to love and serve" the Divine Majesty. Ignatius's Spanish expression "*en todo amar y servir*," expresses simply the dynamic of our retreat. I might note that Ignatius seems to pray for this grace, "to love and to serve in all things," as a summation of the graces of one who is trying to live an Ignatian spirituality.

For those of us familiar with the makeup of the Spiritual Exercises, we are aware that there are some

13

unusual pieces to this Contemplation exercise. First, it is the only exercise for which Ignatius provides us with a prenote. He sets the stage for our appreciation of how people in love act. Ignatius makes two points. In the first point he states that lovers want to express their love more in deeds than in words. In the second point he goes on to say that lovers want to share, each with the other, whatever goods they possess. Ignatius's Spanish word, *comunicar*, which we tend to translate by the English word *share*, underscores the paradox involved in saying that lovers want to express their love more in deeds "than in words." Yet, as Ignatius indicates by his choice of word *comunicar*, every sharing between lovers is meant to "say" something, to "speak."

With these two points of his prenote stated, Ignatius then leads us to reflect how God expresses love. In expressing divine love, what are the ways that God communicates with us? If we listen and then want to respond, what do we say? For the first and only time in the Exercises, Ignatius will suggest his own words as a way of praying by giving us his prayer, *Take and Receive*. Not only is it unusual for Ignatius to give us his way of praying as a possible colloquy response, but he suggests that we might make such a colloquy after each of the four points he suggests for our prayer. We may acknowledge that colloquy (our "praying") may happen anytime within a prayer period. But Ignatius has consistently up to this point in the book noted a colloquy only after the three or five points that he gives for the usual prayer exercise. So both the given prayer form and the encouraged colloquy after *each* point draw special attention to this final prayer exercise.

Some commentators on the Exercises explain the makeup of this final exercise as a review of the Four Week structure. Each point in its own way brings to mind the prayer movements of the respective Weeks. Whether we

14

agree or not with such an interpretation, as we are considering this exercise for prayer on our first day of retreat, we focus our attention on all the ways that God shows and expresses his love for us in our life-story up to this present moment.

We need to reflect: what is our response? Are we able to use Ignatius's suggested words of the *Take and Receive* or do we desire to speak out our own way of making a response?

For a second prayer period, I am suggesting that we consider Ignatius's expression of the Principle and Foundation. I realize that you might say that I am confused or maybe that I am confusing you. I have just suggested that we take the final exercise of the *Spiritual Exercises* first, and then I focus on the first exercise of the retreat as our second exercise of this first day.

Both exercises are dealing with God and with the way God acts. Although Ignatius does not use *love* words in the Principle and Foundation, there is no doubt that he does show us a God who is a Giver of gifts. In fact, a Giver of so many gifts that we must necessarily choose among them. But the important "key" that we have from the Contemplation on the Love of God exercise for our prayer period now on the Principle and Foundation is that "how lovers share *communicates*." And so as we reflect on and ruminate about the Principle and Foundation, what do we find this Giver of all gifts *saying* to us? With the gifts flowing into us in our lives, with the gifts that we have made choices about, what is God saying to us? *That* is where we find ourselves entering into colloquy again in this prayer period.

This first day of retreat I want to have as our context day. Just as Ignatius knew the importance of setting the foundation for the full Exercises, so I believe that it is just as important to allow ourselves to enter into the retreat

15

being familiar with and feeling at home in the context. The context is love, God's love. It is God as lover communicating, speaking to us. So our retreat context given us this first day of retreat is God loving and God speaking. God is first "to love and to serve."

Philip blurted out, "Lord, show us the Father, and that will be enough," and Jesus responded, "Philip, in seeing me you have seen the Father. How can you say 'show us the Father'?" Throughout the following days of the retreat we will be looking at Jesus and we will be coming to know and deepen our relationship with God by expressing our love in the ways we are being called to serve.

For our prayer today, then, I propose that we consider the Ignatian texts:

1) the Contemplation on the Love of God [230-237]
2) the Principle and Foundation [23].

I would suggest that we might take a "ruminating" approach to our prayer periods. Mull over or chew on the text presented by Ignatius. The grace we seek is to listen to how God speaks to us so that in all things we might love and serve God.

Remember our daily mantra: Lord, teach me to be generous. Teach me to serve you as you deserve.

First Day

To Love: A Context of God Speaking

Points:

1. To love is expressed more in deeds than in words. Paradoxically sharing between lovers is meant always to "say" something, to speak.
2. Ignatius reviews the ways that God loves in four ways, perhaps corresponding to our experiences of the Four Weeks of the Exercises, or, more generally, to our life experience.
3. God, the Giver of all good gifts, presented in the Principle and Foundation is speaking to us.

Prayer Texts:

1. the Contemplation on the Love of God, Sp Ex [230]-[237] (see pp. 66-67)
2. the Principle and Foundation, Sp Ex [23] (see p. 68)

Mantra:

Lord, teach me to be generous.
Teach me to serve you as you deserve.

Prayer:

God of all good gifts, be generous to us as we begin this retreat. Let us experience your presence, your power, and your grace. Help us to know your goodness in the many ways that you have gifted us. Draw us close to you so that we can listen even to the most whispered language of your love. Move us to respond to your calls with all our heart.
We ask this in Jesus' name. Amen.

17

An Ignatian Retreat for People Somewhere on the Way

To Serve Is about Following

Prayer

God our Lord, we believe that you have called us into existence. You have called us to share in your Trinitarian life through our baptism. You continue to call us daily that we might be ever more fully enlivened by your love. Help us to be attentive to all the ways that your voice speaks out, your hand beckons us, your eyes invite us. Give us the grace to serve you in our following.

We ask this in Jesus' name. Amen.

To Serve Is about Following

On our first retreat day we were reflecting about God's love and how his way of loving and gifting is also a speaking to us. To love and to serve in all things we rush to apply to ourselves. But God is first to love and to serve. It is God's loving and serving that provide the context of our retreat. Now in these days of our retreat we enter into prayer to understand how we might respond, more like God, in our love and in our service.

For those of us familiar with the makeup of the Ignatian *Spiritual Exercises*, I am intending this shorter retreat to follow more the dynamics found in the Second Week. I will be suggesting scripture passages for our prayer from the public life of Jesus. The grace that I propose for our retreat is that of being drawn more closely to love and serve God our Lord in all things. More specifically we are praying for the grace today to follow the calls of Jesus as our way of loving service.

Wherever we are in our spiritual life shaped by Ignatian spirituality we find ourselves, especially at the time of retreat, asking what more does God want of us. What more can we give? How can we better live as a disciple, a follower, an apostle of the Lord? "What more?" is a question that permeates the life of anyone who is in love.

"What more?" suggests to us the *magis* of Ignatius. *Magis* in Ignatian spirituality makes sense only in the context of love. It does not point to an unsatisfied craving for more work or for a ever-gnawing discontent with our observation of poverty or with an unholy desire for

19

greater accomplishments. The "itch" of the Ignatian *magis* is stimulated by love of Jesus, love of God.

When we observe the public life of Jesus in the Gospels, we should be struck by the way he calls his followers. He just simply calls or invites or says "come and see." Jesus does not first ask what someone has done wrong or demand confession and sorrow for sins committed. He simply says, "Follow." Too often we ourselves try to "clean up our act" and then we say that we will be ready to move forward in our spiritual growth. Perhaps in our ways of ministering or dealing with others, we may find ourselves demanding that they need to go through a lot of self-examination, confessing their sins, and showing signs of their repentance before we are going to talk with them about following Jesus. Perhaps even the Ignatian Exercises themselves have led us to pursue the First Week (often identified as Sin Week) as necessarily and essentially first in our even considering of our following of Jesus.

Yet what do we see in the gospel accounts? We see Jesus calling to Peter and Andrew to follow. And when in the boat with a miraculous catch of fish Peter says "get away from me, for I am a sinful man," all Jesus responds at that time is "you will be fishers of men (and women)." Jesus seems to ignore the confession of Peter as not relevant at this time. The focus fixed by Jesus at the beginning of Peter's call and again in the post-resurrection questioning of Peter is always the same: "Follow."

In that word *follow* is the "more," the *magis*, for Peter, for Andrew, and for all of us disciples. How do we describe "to follow"? Are *we* the ones *doing* anything? "To follow" demands of us a kind of active passivity. We are *following*. For us disciples of Jesus, "to follow" remains an essential part of what it means for us to serve.

When Jesus calls Matthew, the tax collector, Matthew

follows. But Matthew's response is nothing like Peter's, with his saying "get away from me, for I am a sinful man." Rather Matthew is so enthused and excited about his being invited to the "more" that he wants to celebrate with a party. Evidently the party caused a stir among the towns-people since Matthew invited his "kind" of friends—other tax collectors and people who did not observe the Jewish laws and regulations. And there was Jesus sitting in the midst of them, enjoying the party. Unlike Zacchaeus, in another gospel story, we do not hear Matthew saying that he has done anything wrong or that he is going to be giving any money back. His eyes seem to be fixed on following Jesus. What more was necessary!

What we seem to find in the Gospels, then, is Jesus entering into people's lives and inviting them to follow him—right from where they are, from boats and fishnets and from tax booths. He does not demand first that they run to the synagogue (or in our modern equivalent the church or the confessional). Jesus' call is the first of the "what more's" in our life. There will be many more, per-haps rightly said, an infinite number more. But the call of Jesus, every time we look at it and hear it and try to respond, is the *magis* call. Our response, our service, is "to follow."

Our attention this second day of retreat, then, is on the call of Jesus as we contemplate it in gospel incidents, and the response of people "to follow." I am suggesting that we enter into the gospel passage in the way tradi-tional to Ignatian contemplation—com-posing ourselves (not just a composition of place only, but *our* com-posi-tion) in the scene, seeing the people, listening to what they say, watching what they do. We are there, and then, as Ignatius indicates, we do what we do, say what we say. Colloquy, or our prayer response, happens whenever the grace of God moves us to speak out.

21

I am suggesting two passages, and I would encourage a repetition or two, if you are determining for yourself (or with a director) that you desire three or four prayer periods in your day. I just remind you that an Ignatian repetition does not focus upon a repeat of the matter, the scripture passage. The repetition looks to those moments of consolation or desolation that you have noted down after your examen of the preceding contemplations. You enter into your repetition prayer through your consolations and desolations.

Today I propose the scripture passage from Luke 5:1-11, the account of the call to Peter and Andrew and Peter's response. The second passage is the call of Matthew found in Matthew 9:9-13.

The grace we seek today: that we may be graced with the simple action of following the calls of Jesus in our lives as our way of loving service.

Remember our mantra: "Lord, teach me to be generous. Teach me to serve you as you deserve."

Second Day

To Serve Is about Following

Points:

1. Jesus' call to follow, as we find it in the gospels, precedes any confession of sin or wrongdoing on the part of the people called.

2. Jesus' call to follow takes people where they are.

3. The call "to follow" is a *magis* call.

Prayer Texts:

1. Luke 5:1-11, the call of Peter and Andrew and Peter's response

2. Matthew 9:9-13, the call of Matthew and Matthew's response

Mantra:

Lord, teach me to be generous.
Teach me to serve you as your deserve.

Prayer:

God our Lord, we believe that you have called us into existence. You have called us to share in your Trinitarian life through our baptism. You continue to call us daily that we might be ever more fully enlivened by your love. Help us to be attentive to all the ways that your voice speaks out, your hand beckons, and your eyes invite us. Give us the grace to serve you in our following.

We ask this in Jesus' name. Amen.

An Ignatian Retreat for People Somewhere on the Way

To Serve Is about Availability

Prayer

Lord God, you know that we can be busy about many things. We want to do good deeds for your praise and glory, but we get focused on our own accomplishments. Help us, we pray, to let go of our busyness and to experience an availability to you. Let us come into your presence, with this prayer on our lips: Lord, we stand ready and willing.

We make this prayer in Jesus' name. Amen.

Three
To Serve Is about Availability

We have been examining the Ignatian expression "in all (things) to love and to serve." We are focusing on "to serve" with all the richness of its meanings. Yesterday we focused just on the call. What a gift—so free in its expression—is the call of Jesus, however many times it happens in our lives. Then there is the focus on our freedom of "following" which becomes our acting out of the meaning of *servir*, "to serve." The call and the following are all tied together in the Ignatian sense of *magis* or "more." Just "to follow" is an action responding to the question "what more?" implied in each call of Christ in our lives.

On the feast of the Assumption of Our Lady, we Jesuits commemorate the occasion of the vow of Ignatius and his first companions in a little chapel at Montmartre in Paris in 1534. The vow was to spend their lives in service of the Lord in the Holy Land. *That* vow of service was never to be fulfilled. Some three years later after they had all been ordained to the priesthood, they renewed this vow of their own pre-determined service in the Holy Land, but, they added, barring the realization of this vow, they had an alternative. They would make themselves *available* to mission by the pope. It is important for us to note that God took them up on this alternative for service. Today I would like us to pray about *availability* as a way of serving.

Let me begin with a simple example. What makes for a good waiter in a restaurant? It is not that this waiter is always hovering over our table, doing things like top-

25

ping off a water glass or sweeping up some crumbs. Most of us get annoyed when a waiter hovers over us and gives us too much attention. The good waiter is the one who is always available, who watches, pays attention, and is always there when needed. This waiter brings home to us the adage "he also serves who only stands and waits."

I would propose that we consider how Jesus elicits responses from people in the Gospels. We all are familiar with the story of the one we have consistently identified as the "rich young man." He is identified only in one passing reference in Matthew's Gospel as "young," but perhaps we so readily identify him because we think of his idealism as a part of youth. He is one who asks "what more, what further do I need to do?" In both Matthew and Mark, he is identified only as "a man came up" or "a man came running up and knelt before him." In Luke he is signalized as "one of the ruling class." Perhaps the "ruling class" implies a background of wealth, and Luke further on designates him as "a very rich man." Both Matthew and Mark, while not initially indicating him as rich, picture him turning away from Jesus because he had "many possessions." Mark has the most touching detail in his story when he notes that Jesus "looked at him with love."

The story is a simple one. A person comes to Jesus and asks what more can he do to gain eternal life. Jesus, being the good Jew he is, reminds him of the commandments, emphasizing the ones of human interaction: you shall not kill, you shall not commit adultery, you shall not steal, you shall not bear false witness, honor your father and your mother, and then Jesus adds from the book of Deuteronomy, love your neighbor as yourself. The man seems disappointed at this commonplace, almost catechism-like, answer. And he protests that he has kept all these commandments from his youth. He is asking what more can he do to gain eternal life. It is at this point in the story that Mark notes that Jesus looks upon him with love. The man must not have been boastful; he really is a good man, and Jesus' heart is captivated by his youthful goodness.

Jesus presents the man with the challenge he asked for. Jesus does not immediately say "follow," as in the case of the first apostles. In our story today, Jesus asks this person, who is so eager to serve, for something more. Jesus challenges him and us to be free of what we claim as our own—our possessions, things dear to us like our own ideas and our own wants and desires. Then, freed from all these "things," we may find ourselves unencumbered in our ability to serve however Jesus may want to shape our desires and our dreams. While following is a form of service, as we have prayed to be so graced in our previous reflection, another way of serving is our "being available."

The young man, for all his idealism, failed in his imagining that he could ever live so free as just "to be available" to Jesus. We might want to ask him: what is it that he felt that he had to have, what dreams or desires was he unwilling to let go of, which would prevent him from being free and available for Jesus? Whatever it was, he experienced it as something that made him sad. From our Ignatian perspective, we would say that he needed St. Ignatius to help him sort out what made him feel sad and desolate, and what excited him and made him feel alive. But after asking his own question "What more?," he went away sad because he chose not to respond.

Just "being available" is a hard stance for us to maintain as a way of serving. And yet good service, service of God, divine service—like good table waiting—demands people who are available. This young man may have done many jobs for Jesus, if only Jesus had asked him to do "a

27

job." But just being available was too hard for him. To serve, by being available, is not easy. Jesus knows about the "many things" that hold us back from just being available as our stance of service.

The second story I alluded to yesterday. It is the story of the little man Zacchaeus. He is short of stature, and yet he wanted to see this famous preacher Jesus. He could not see over the heads of the crowds, and so he climbed a tree. Now we are told that Zacchaeus is the *chief* tax collector (seemingly more important in his position than Matthew is) and a wealthy man. In any culture and at any time, people important with titles and with money do not make fools of themselves by climbing trees, like young boys. What would seem to make Zacchaeus's position in the tree even worse comes from Jesus' looking up and seeing him and then, in front of all the people surrounding him, Jesus calls to Zacchaeus to hurry and come down so that he can spend time at his house. However foolish he may have felt, Zacchaeus was totally focused on Jesus' request: "He wants to spend time at my house."

It seems that in the gospels tax collectors and, in general, sinners love to give banquets, and Jesus accepts the invitation to be present. Does Jesus expressing his desire to Zacchaeus that "I want to stay at your house" really call him, not just to follow, but to change his way of living? We know that Zacchaeus does change his way of life, going well beyond just being honest and good. He says, "I give half my belongings to the poor, and if I have defrauded anyone, I pay him back fourfold." Whereas Jesus had given instruction to the rich young man about divesting himself and becoming unencumbered, it appears that Zacchaeus himself was moved to share what he had with those who did not have. If he had done some wrong things, he would make up for it fourfold—in other words, way beyond what is called for by justice and, perhaps,

28

even charity. For Zacchaeus, the service of his new relationship with Jesus embraces a change of life that has no
preconditions, that just allows him to be available, to let
Jesus stay at his house. Like Zacchaeus, if we allow Jesus
to stay in our house, we will find ourselves being more
available.

For our prayer time, I propose that we might use the
rich young man passage from Luke 18:18-43. You will
find its parallel passage in Mark 10:17-27 and Matthew
19:16-22. Again I encourage you to enter into your prayer
through Ignatian contemplation—seeing and hearing and
watching.

For your second prayer period, we would consider
Luke 19:1-11 which allows us to enter into the story of
Zacchaeus. And depending on whether you are planning
on three or four periods of prayer, I suggest that the other
periods be used in true Ignatian repetition.

The grace we seek is: the grace of being available as
our way of serving.

Our mantra: "Lord, teach me to be generous. Teach
me to serve you as you deserve."

An Ignatian Retreat for People Somewhere on the Way

To Serve Is about Availability

Points:

1. Jesus' call is to sell, to give, to come, to follow.

2. Jesus' desire is "to spend time at my house."

3. To serve means being available.

Prayer Texts:

1. Luke 18:18-43, the young man of the ruling class

2. Luke 19:1-11, the story of Zacchaeus

Mantra:

> Lord, teach me to be generous.
> Teach me to serve you as you deserve.

Prayer:

> Lord God, you know that we can be busy about many things. We want to do good deeds for your praise and glory, but we get focused on our own accomplishments. Help us, we pray, to let go of our busyness and to experience an availability to you. Let us come into your presence, with this prayer on our lips: Lord, we stand ready and willing.
>
> We ask this in Jesus' name. Amen.

To Serve Is to Believe

Prayer

God ever faithful and true, we feel weak and lacking in faith. You know that we say our prayers and we celebrate the Eucharist, but we confess that our bodies and souls are there, not our hearts. Give us a double portion of your Spirit, just as your prophet Elisha prayed. Make our faith firm so that we are confirmed in your service.

We ask this in Jesus' name. Amen.

To Serve Is to Believe

As we continue to consider our following of Jesus, we are impressed by the fact that the question continues to arise for us, "what more?," every time we interact with Jesus. That is what all his followers experienced. His close followers knew his call and his continuing invitations to something more. And the "something more" every time fills out our understanding of what it means to serve.

A common, chiding complaint of Jesus in the gospels is our lack of faith. "O you of little faith," "why are you lacking in faith?" "where is your faith?"—expressions from the beginning of Jesus' public ministry all the way to the incident of doubting Thomas after the resurrection. Remember that God is the first to love and to serve. God puts a lot of faith in us; God believes in us, God believes us. Essential to serving is our believing in God, our believing God. As we work with others, we serve by believing in them, by believing them.

A lot of good works are done, even by us Catholics, but the works truly do not merit the identity of service, "to serve God in all things." Why not? Because "to serve" is grounded in "to believe." God works through faith-filled people. They are servants of God. Our first service is to have faith, to believe. Our first way of serving God is to believe in God. Our first way of serving others is to believe in them, as sons and daughters of God. Teilhard de Chardin once wrote "you cannot convert what you do not love." To expand on this truth, we cannot serve what we do not believe in. There is an age-old tradition that an essential requirement to be a theologian is that

33

one must pray. "To pray" in other words is "to believe." The first service of a theologian is that he or she serves us, the church, by being a believer. Only then does the theologian serve us by his or her theologizing in teaching or in writing.

If I may make a reference to the religious life of Jesuits, Ignatius is famous for his stress on obedience as an essential of Jesuit life and mission. Ignatius grants that there is an obedience of execution, that is, one being told to do a job and one obeys and does it. A good work is done, but is it service? Does it serve God? Ignatius calls for more in his spirituality. Obedience must be infused with faith for service. To serve God is to believe.

Today I want to present a couple of gospel passages that expand our way of looking at "to serve" through a challenge about our depth of believing. To serve the Lord demands an ever deepening faith in God, in God's love and care and personal concern, in God's working. The "what more" of our being ready to serve lies in the challenging growth of our response to believe.

The first gospel passage I suggest is Mark 5:35-41, the incident of the storm at sea. Jesus had finished an exhausting day of teaching the crowds of people following him. As the day was almost over, he says to the apostles that he would like them all to get in boats and go across to the farther shore. While they were underway, one of those sudden, but violent, wind and rainstorms blew up. The sea was roiled up so that the waves were crashing over the side of the boat. When someone is totally exhausted, it is amazing how much it might take to wake a person up. Likely this is the situation for Jesus. But I think that we also have another truth evident here. Jesus so literally sleeps in the arms of God his Father—the One he serves—that the comfort and security level he feels holds him in peaceful sleep.

And so the men in the boat with him, as they are trying to bail out the water that is breaking over the side of the boat, cry out to him. "Wake up, don't you worry about all of us capsizing and going down with the boat?' And then Jesus stands up in the boat which is rolling from side to side and says "Be still." And with that, the winds die down and the waves become a slowly moderating swell.

Then Jesus looks at his companions, and he simply questions, "Why were you so afraid? Why don't you relax in your faith? Why don't you let your faith lead you on? Why do you have so little faith?" If these followers of Jesus, these apostles, were to carry Jesus to another shore, to different people, how could they serve him—carrying him to others—if they had little faith? Just "to believe" is to serve.

Our second passage is from the gospel of Matthew: Matthew 17:14-20, the incident of the possessed boy. The timing of this story is that it follows immediately upon the incident of Jesus' transfiguration experienced by Peter, James, and John. The four of them are coming down from the mountain, and immediately a man runs up to Jesus and begs him to help his demented son. This son who seems to thrown himself into fires or else into the waters of rivers or wells was taken to Jesus' disciples, but they seemingly could do nothing.

We may be surprised by Jesus' reaction. He speaks out his obvious frustration with his complaint, "How long can I endure a people so lacking in faith?" Jesus appears to be referring to his followers. And so, with the boy in front of him, Jesus immediately cures him.

Now, the disciples, feeling a little sheepish, approach Jesus and ask, "Why couldn't we help this boy? Remember you had sent us out to heal the sick and to drive out demons." And Jesus looked long at them and said, "You know it's not magic. It isn't something *you* do. You need

35

to keep growing in faith. Always beg God the Father to increase your faith, small as a mustard seed though it may be."

Today we explore how our faith is what allows us to live with God, to rest in God, no matter the situations around us. It is an ever growing faith that allows us to be people who can be of service.

We also acknowledge that it is only if we pray that God increase our faith that we can be God's instruments in whatever way God may want to use us. God can only work in and through us if we are faith-filled. Perhaps we should especially pray to Mary. We say "Mary, full of grace"; we can also say "Mary, full of faith." Can we name great deeds or works that Mary has done? It is not in great deeds or accomplishments that we see Mary as servant of God, but in the fact that she is faith-filled. Pray through Mary that our service comes from our being "faith-filled."

To help us, then, in our praying about being the kind of servants who are growing in faith, I propose for our first prayer period: Mark 4:35-41. And for our second prayer period, I propose Matthew 17:14-20. Again I would encourage that our method of entering into the Gospel passages be through Ignatian contemplation of seeing the persons, listening to what they say, and watching their actions. The repetitions, too, should follow the Ignatian directive of not repeating the material, but to return to those places where we found consolation or desolation.

The grace we pray for is: that we may be people who serve just by the depth of our lived faith.

Our mantra: "Lord, teach me to be generous. Teach me to serve you as you deserve."

Fourth Day

To Serve Is to Believe

Points:

1. To believe is to rest in the arms of God.

2. God's grace is always present for us to grow in faith.

3. God sees our service as a people who are faith-filled.

Prayer Texts:

1. Mark 4:35-41, Jesus and the storm at sea

2. Matthew 17:14-20, the possessed boy

Mantra:

Lord, teach me to be generous.
Teach me to serve you as your deserve.

Prayer:

God ever faithful and true, we feel weak and lacking in faith. You know that we say our prayers and we celebrate Eucharist, but we confess that often our bodies and souls are there, not our hearts. Give us a double portion of your Spirit, just as your prophet Elisha prayed. Make our faith firm so that we can be confirmed in your service.

We ask this in Jesus' name. Amen.

37

To Serve Is about Accompaniment

Prayer

Good and gracious God, you created us as a human family. In Jesus, you invite us into your own divine life as our Trinitarian God. Just as Jesus' arms on the cross are spread wide to embrace you and all of us, help us open wide our arms in welcoming you and all our brothers and sisters. Enliven this grace within us: that being together and working together we might enter more fully into your service.

We ask this in Jesus' name. Amen.

To Serve Is about Accompaniment

As we enter into this day of the retreat, we continue to hear our question, "What more, Jesus, may you be asking of us?" How are we to understand what it means for us to serve?

In the meditation "The Call of the King" which begins the Second Week of the Spiritual Exercises, Ignatius presents the contemporary risen Christ making his call to every man, woman, and child to follow him. Christ invites all to be with him in his experiences, even those hard and demanding, because the goal—life forever with God—is assured. What Ignatius emphasizes throughout his text in the words of Jesus is *comigo*, the Spanish expression for "with me." Jesus calls us to be *with* him. He wants us to work *with* him. He desires us to share the victory of resurrection *with* him.

What may not be so evident is that in Jesus' inviting everyone to follow and be with him, all of us, his followers, are put into relation with one another. We are with one another in being with Jesus, all of us companions brought together by him. We are with one another in working with Jesus, all of us companions about the one mission, the mission to which Jesus calls us. The Christian mission, then, can never be seen as an individualistic one, even though there are those moments when a person may seem to be very alone and unique in his or her Christian calling. We always interact as cells within the Body of Christ, and the healthiness of the cells or members is from their very interworking.

We come, then, to another understanding of what it

means for us to serve. We must be in relationship. To serve is "to be with" and "to work with." We acknowledge first that we must be in relationship with Christ.

What does it mean for us to be in relationship with Christ? We call Christ "our redeemer." For many of us, the word *redeemer* may find its meaning in its Latin roots of "buying back." *Redeemer* and *redemption* sound very mercenary or business-like. *Redeemer* finds its Hebrew root in the word *go'el*. *Go'el* means a kin person, one who is a blood relationship. In any difficulty, we could always depend on the *go'el* to help because we are all part of the family. I believe that it is the prophet Isaiah who first applies the Hebrew word *go'el*, "redeemer," to God. In Jesus—God become human—we truly have God as *go'el*, redeemer. But Jesus enters us further into the meaning. He not only shares our human blood, but he shares his divine self with us in baptism and Eucharist. God not only identifies with us in Jesus in our human family, but in Jesus' sharing of his Body and his Blood and in his gifting of the Spirit we find ourselves all part of God's family, the Trinitarian life.

We also realize that in Christ we find ourselves in a plethora of relationships throughout our lives because of our Christian calling. We find ourselves in our family origins, we develop friendships, we may have the special relationship of marriage, we perhaps find ourselves in the bonds of religious community or in the brotherhood of priests. We all are in relationship, within the Body of Christ. To be in relationship is the only way to serve Christ, to serve God.

40

I have already alluded to St. Paul, with his description of the Body of Christ. Let us listen to the words of Paul as he makes concrete through images the relationship that is ours. As St. Paul says in chapter 12 of his first letter to the Corinthians:

If a foot should say "Because I am not a hand, I do not belong to the body," it does not for this reason belong any less to the body. Or if an ear should say, "Because I am not an eye, I do not belong to the body," it does not for this reason belong any less to the body. If the whole body were an eye, where would the hearing be? If the whole body were hearing, were would the sense of smell be? . . . The eye cannot say to the hand, "I do not need you" nor again the head to the feet "I do not need you." . . . If one part suffers, all the parts suffer with it; if one part is honored, all the parts share its joy.

St. Paul could not be more dramatic in describing how we all are always in relationship.

We also might look at St. Ignatius Loyola in his own growth. It is interesting to watch Ignatius the pilgrim, leaving Manresa, seemingly with the desire to spend his life in service in the Holy Land *by himself.* When that idea is aborted by the Franciscan guardians responsible for the Christian sites, Ignatius has to believe that God is directing him in another way. When he determines to study in order to better serve, he seems also to feel led by God to serve with others. His first attempt to gather companions was a failure in Spain. But in Paris God gives him his companions. Serving, we note for Ignatius, as he describes it in his *Autobiography*, has expanded its meaning, just as we have been praying about it in this retreat. For Ignatius, "following" is the grace at Loyola; "availability" becomes his grace at Manresa; "believing" is the grace tested and accepted in his pilgrim time. Now at Paris he is receiving the grace of being in relationship. When Ignatius and the companions make themselves available to the pope for individual mission, they realize that a discernment is called for—a discernment on the part of the total group of the companions. Do they want to serve together, serving as members of a Body? The answer is yes, and the result

41

is the religious body of companions called the Company of Jesus, the Society of Jesus.

Let us turn to a couple of scripture passages to let this notion of service as relationship come home to our heart more fully.

I propose that first we take Mark 5:1-20, the incident of Jesus dealing with the Gerasene demoniac. For some time I personally considered this gospel story a bit bizarre, and I would hesitate to make use of it for retreats or days of recollection. Now I find it a very rich and evocative passage for prayer.

The picture that we get of this man is frightening. He is uncontrolled and uncontrollable. Whatever restraints had been tried, he has broken them. So he is exiled. He lives outside the village—among tombs where only dead people are. It seems that he screams out and carries on day and night and mistreats his own body, gashing himself with stones.

Jesus had no sooner got out of the boat than this possessed man is running towards him, screaming out for Jesus to get away and stop meddling with him. We need to recognize the paradox of a man running towards Jesus and at the same time screaming about his staying away. Jesus, in the face of this mad man rushing at him, seems to be quietly praying "Unclean spirit, come out of the man!" And then Jesus asks the man, "What is your name?" The man stops, and out of his mouth come the words "Legion is my name. There are hundreds of us." Then there is this strange bargaining of these spirits with Jesus to let them stay in the neighborhood.

Since we are outside Jewish territory, there is a large herd of swine (in the Jewish eyes an unclean animal not to be dealt with). These dark spirits beg to be allowed to enter the swine. Jesus gives the okay, and the spirits immediately come out of the man and enter into the herd

42

of swine. Lo and behold, the swine go rushing down the hillside into the lake where they drown. The swineherders run to town to tell the owners and the people what had happened to their swine.

When the townspeople came to Jesus, they found this man sitting quietly, clothed like normal people, and quite sane. All these goings-on was too much for these people—they lost their swine by some strange happening and even stranger is this crazy man sitting calmly before them, now so ordinary again, just like themselves. Their response is: get this Jewish prophet/miracle worker out of our territory. And so Jesus was going towards the boat to leave, and the man, once so mean and destructive, wants to accompany Jesus.

And, surprise, Jesus does not grant his request. This man was not a Jew. Jesus rather gives him a different invitation: to go home to his family and share with them how good God has been to him. The man does become an "apostle"—proclaiming all that Jesus has done for him—in non-Jewish territory.

We see here a man in relationship with Jesus—not in company with him like the Twelve, but one alive with the "new life" which Jesus had shared with him. Jesus encourages his relationship with family and friends, and the man himself seems to extend his relationships in an apostolic way to people living in various cities—the ten cities grouped as the Decapolis. He is *with* Jesus, and he continues to *work with* Jesus in his proclaiming good news. We need to go beyond the gospel accounts. We can readily imagine that he calls family and friends to work with him to proclaim the power of God from his own witness of life and to celebrate this God's presence for us as the God of all our lives.

The second passage we will use for our prayer is Mark 3:31-35, the passage about Jesus and his family. Jesus is in a house, and the crowds around him listening to his teachings do not allow for anyone to go in or out. His mother and some family members come along—in this passage we are not told why they are seeking Jesus, though in other places we are told that his relatives thought that he might be going crazy or at least suffering from nervous exhaustion, and they wanted him to come home. Since they cannot get into the house because of the crowds, they send word that "your mother and your brothers and sisters are outside asking for you."

Jesus looks around at the people before him and he asks "Who are my mother and my brothers?" Immediately he answers his own question: "Whoever does the will of God is brother and sister and mother to me."

Jesus emphasizes that to *be with* him is to *act like* him. Being in relationship with Jesus means to "work with" him in being available to what God wants—doing God's will. This gospel passage inspires Ignatius in his picturing the risen Christ issuing his call to be with him and to labor with him so as to enjoy the victory of the Kingdom of God with him, to accomplish God's will. The gospel passage we may feel is all too short. But it contains a depth of meaning for Jesus' listeners and for us. In your prayer, you may want also to return with Ignatius to his own "Call of the King" meditation.

For our Ignatian contemplation I suggest that we pray the gospel passages from Mark 5:1-20 and Mark 3:31-35. How better might we, together with others, serve the Lord? What more in our relationships is Christ asking of us at this time?

The grace we desire: the grace to be in relationship with Jesus and with others as our way of serving.

Our mantra: "Lord, teach me to be generous. Teach me to serve you as you deserve."

Fifth Day

To Serve Is about Accompaniment

Points:

1. To serve is "to be with" and "to work with."

2. In Jesus, we are always members, cells,
    working together within the Body.

3. In Jesus, we are in a blood relationship with God
    and with every other human being.

Prayer Texts:

1. Mark 5:1-20, the Gerasene demoniac

2. Mark 3:31-35, Jesus and his family

Mantra:

Lord, teach me to be generous.
Teach me to serve you as you deserve.

Prayer:

Good and gracious God, you created us as a human
family. In Jesus, you invite us into your own divine life
as our Trinitarian God. Just as Jesus' arms on the cross
are spread wide to embrace you and all of us, help us
to open wide our arms in welcoming you and all our
brothers and sisters. Enliven this grace within us: that
being together and working together we might enter
more fully into your service.
   We ask this in Jesus' name. Amen.

45

To Serve Is about Forgiveness

Prayer

Compassionate God, we know you as the father who rushes out to welcome his wayward son back home. You not only extend arms to embrace, offer a kiss, clothe in finery, but also celebrate your forgiving love with a banquet. Give us your grace so that as we progress in our love for you and for our neighbor, we also grow in your way of forgiveness. Forgive us the wrongs we have done and help us to forgive those who have wronged us. Let forgiveness and compassion mark our loving service of you.

We ask this in Jesus' name. Amen.

Six To Serve Is about Forgiveness

Each day of this retreat we are listening to God in order to be able to give ourselves over more fully to his direction. Our continuing question is the "what more?" of someone who is trying to express love. Love is seen in our way of acting, the way we serve.

We are deepening in our sense of what it means for us to serve. Each time, of course, we find ourselves being challenged to grow in our way of loving. It seems to me that Jesus continues to draw people close to himself, in the gospels especially the Twelve, sending them out on mission, asking them to do what he does. They are pictured as having a number of successes, and a few setbacks. As their closeness with Jesus develops and as they try to act in the way that Jesus acts, they also realize how they can be self-focused, how they can want to get ahead and be special, how they can be self-righteous, and eventually how they can run away and even betray. And so another understanding of serving is being born in them—accepting forgiveness and being enabled to forgive.

The picture of followers in the gospels remains true for us followers today. Yes, there can be a sense of sin and the need for forgiveness at an early point in our lives as we want to be free of the sins we commit and we resolve to get serious about our relationship with God. But it seems that as we grow in our life experience, we also grow in our sensitivity of how often we can in little ways wrong God and others and how often and in little ways people, even those who love us, can wrong us. Our sense of how sin pervades our lives and our sincerity in seeking forgiveness

47

and our readiness to forgive others increase the more we grow as loving persons. Contrary to how we often image progress in the spiritual life, sinning and seeking forgiveness loom larger for those more acutely sensitive of love and its costs. We have hint of this in the different grace that we pray for by Ignatius's directions in the First Week of the Spiritual Exercises and the grace prayed for in the Third Week. It is the difference expressed between asking for "shame and confusion" in the First Week and asking for "grief, feeling, and confusion" in the Third Week. Shame, with its focus on self and our wrong-doing is no longer a grace sought. In the grace of the Third Week, how we serve God (Jesus) is by our compassion.

For example, the sacrament of reconciliation can take on a richer and deeper meaning for persons growing in love and in service than it does for persons who are just coming to free themselves from gross sinful actions and habits of sin. The early-on sinner in the process of conversion feels the burdens of the evil he or she has done and has the sense of getting out from under the weight of sin. The one growing in love is pained by his or her own betrayal of love he or she has committed and is warmed by the embrace of compassionate love in return. As the prodigal son felt it, so we can feel a grief and confusion still in the face of such compassionate love from God or from another person. Perhaps for us people somewhere on the way in our spiritual lives, confession may more likely be appropriate towards the end of a retreat or even sometime thereafter. We have sharpened our love sensitivities and so more readily see our faults and seek forgiveness. To know forgiveness and to be able to forgive is central for us as a way of serving.

Let us consider the gospel passage Luke 7:36-50.. The scene is Jesus being at table as a guest of Simon the Pharisee. A woman, known as a public sinner (which bluntly translates as a prostitute), makes her way into the house and kneels behind Jesus as he reclines at table. Prostitution is a reality in the gospels, as it seems to be in every culture. It is also a symbol often in the Old Testament, particularly in the psalms and in the prophets, of all of us as sinners. All sin is prostitution. We sell our love to someone or something as a choice against God.

This woman is washing his feet with her tears, drying them with her hair, and then kissing his feet and perfuming them. Now the Pharisee host is thinking to himself that this guest of his is really not the prophet that he is made out to be. Jesus decides that this is a teaching moment. Jesus tells a story about two people owing money to a money-lender. He involves Simon in judging who would be the more grateful with their unequal debts forgiven. With Simon's honest response, Jesus then makes application to what this woman has been doing. It is a question of forgiveness, but Jesus identifies it as coming forth especially from its roots in love. Jesus, the one expressing forgiveness, loves this woman, and the woman, the one experiencing forgiveness, loves Jesus and expresses her love not in words but in deeds—deeds which speak. Jesus speaks words of forgiveness to this woman and encourages her in her faith. We witness the service of offering forgiveness and the service of accepting forgiveness.

We will take for our second gospel passage John 21: 15-22. There is the dialogue interplay between Peter and Jesus. Forgiveness is never mentioned; the conversation is about love. But Jesus, Peter, and we are aware that the context is Peter's denial that he even knew this Jesus the Galilean and ultimately his action of deserting, running away, from the crucifixion of Jesus. Peter lives with what he has done. But Jesus reaches out as always with a question of "what more?"

49

Jesus' first question of Peter on this morning after the resurrection is a "more" question. Jesus asks Peter whether Peter loves him (Jesus) more than these. The word *these* is a bit enigmatic. It is doubtful that Jesus is referring to Peter's love of fishing, his boats, and so on. Jesus could be asking Peter whether he (Peter) loves Jesus more than he loves his family, his brother Andrew, and the rest of his fishing companions. Jesus could also be asking Peter whether he (Peter) loves Jesus more than Peter's companions (the rest of the Apostles) love Jesus. How bold and impetuous will Peter once again be if he is to say that "I, Peter, love you, Jesus, more than my companions love you"? But wonderful Peter, the one among all those who ran away except for John, the one who publicly denied even knowing Jesus three times when asked or accused—this same Peter can meekly say "Yes." Then he adds immediately, "Lord, you know how I love, how much I love." Peter seems to say "I really do love you, Lord, despite how sometimes I have acted. In fact, if I could be so bold, I think that I love you more than these other fellows, my companions, love you. But who am I to say? You know our hearts. You know better than I what kind of love is inside me." Again we see a loving forgiveness being offered as Jesus serves Peter, and Peter's fumbling "yes" is his humbly accepting Jesus' compassionate love.

We each must enter into the scene through Ignatian contemplation. Perhaps Jesus nods his head, says, "Feed my lambs," and some time in silence passes. Then Jesus asks a second time: "Do you love me?" Peter may feel his own heart skip a beat, and he yet more chastenedly repeats his same answer. And Jesus nods, says "Feed my sheep," and again there passes a quiet time. Then comes that same question once more. Peter this time, with a little bit of hurt desperation in his voice, says plainly, "Lord, you know everything. You know that deep down I do love you." And Jesus not only repeats "Feed my sheep," but adds a challenge about Peter's future and then closes the conversation with "Follow me." The gifts given to us by God are the gifts that we are to share with others. The forgiving love of God which Peter has been given must become his way of serving others.

Peter is learning one of the richest lessons about being one who serves. We cannot change the past wrongs we have done; we can only open our hearts and accept forgiveness. And if we receive forgiveness, then we must be empowered to offer forgiveness to others. This is the gift that Jesus had offered on that first Easter evening to the Apostles—all of whom had failed him—and so their first need was for Jesus to serve them, not by washing feet, but by offering forgiveness. And if they were to receive forgiveness, then they must be able to serve others by forgiving. Through the apostles on this first Easter evening, we all, the church, have been called to the service of forgiveness. One of the most wonderful signs of our growing as loving persons is our desire to seek forgiveness for however we may have hurt our relationship with another and our compassion in forgiving the wrongs and slights of others. To seek forgiveness and to be forgiving grounds our service of God who serves us in being compassionate and forgiving. We want to serve as God serves us. We want to grow in our compassion for ourselves and in our compassion for others.

For our prayer time, then, I propose the gospel passage from Luke 7:36-50. For the second passage I offer John 21: 15-22. May our contemplations and our repetitions deepen our appreciation of forgiveness as a way of serving.

The grace we pray for is: the grace to grow in our sensitivity to seek forgiveness from God and from others and to grow as forgiving and compassionate persons ourselves.

Our mantra: "Lord, teach me to be generous. Teach me to serve you as you deserve."

Sixth Day

To Serve Is about Forgiveness

Points:

1. Our sensitivity in seeking forgiveness and in our forgiving grows stronger and becomes more intense as we grow in our love relationship with Jesus.

2. Seeking forgiveness is expressed both in word and in deed.

3. If our lives are permeated by forgiveness, God can entrust us with his mission of compassion.

Prayer Texts:

1. Luke 7:36-50, the penitent woman

2. John 21:15-22, Jesus questioning Peter

Mantra:

Lord, teach me to be generous.
Teach me to serve you as you deserve.

Prayer:

Compassionate God, we know you as the father who rushes out to welcome his wayward son back home. You not only extend arms to embrace, offer a kiss, clothe in finery, but also celebrate your forgiving love with a banquet. Give us your grace so that as we progress in our love for you and for our neighbor, we also grow in your way of forgiveness. Forgive us the wrongs we have done and help us to forgive those who have wronged us. Let forgiveness and compassion mark our loving service of you.

To Serve Is Sharing

Prayer

Ever bountiful God, you lavish your gifts upon us. Even more, you so identify yourself with us that Jesus is your Son enfleshed in our human family. Yet even taking on our human nature forever in his risen life, Jesus promised us a second Paraclete, a Gift of your life always within us. You share with us your Spirit, the love bond of your Trinitarian Being. Love poured out is your way of serving us. Grant us the grace to respond to your love by our own life of sharing. May your Spirit strengthen us in our desire to live a life that is marked by a love poured out.

We ask this in Jesus' name. Amen.

Seven
To Serve Is Sharing

As we continue to pray about our serving, we realize that serving is a rich and inclusive word. The richness of the expression "to serve" comes from its association with the expression "to love." Because of its relation to loving, serving finds its continuing questioning of "what more?" As we continue to pray about our ways of serving the Lord, we clarify for ourselves the many faces that our serving takes on.

Today we want to consider how much our desire to share, our willingness to share, is a way of our serving. We may not so readily want to share our giftedness and our consolations from God. We are tempted to hold them to ourselves as if they were under our control or some-how were our creation or production. And yet as Ignatius reminds us in his prenote to the Contemplation on the Love of God, it is a mark of a lover to want to share what she or he has been given. Just as serving flows from love, so sharing becomes a way of serving.

I have often wondered at how often people are afraid to pray Ignatius's prayer "Take and Receive." The expression, "take all my memory, my understanding, my entire will," appears extreme to them and puts them off from praying. Do we really want God to take our memory, our understanding, and our ability to choose? Are we ready for God to take them? And so it happens that people, even at the end of a thirty-day retreat, may find this prayer too much for them. Yet Ignatius has already given us his way of understanding this prayer and so enabling us to make it our own. In his prenote to the Contemplation, he has said that lovers share. Lovers do not take or remove anything. They only share.

Let us take for our first scripture passage Mark 10:35-45. This is the passage where James and John are asking Jesus for the places on each side of him. We might interpret their request as their wanting to be important. But we also might hear their request as a desire to be really close to Jesus, and, to their way of thinking, if closeness brings some privileges, all the better. We are presented with a picture of two men who may have a mix of motives—just as we often have a similar confusion when it comes to why we do what we do. When Jesus challenges them about whether they are willing to face the demands of what they seek, they impetuously say "yes." Then Jesus assures them that they will pay the costs of loving, for that is what they are truly seeking. But he cannot promise them how close their love brings them to him or to God. God's continuing gift of grace in our lives and our response to grace given is what determines our life's goal—union with God forever.

Immediately the other apostles become aware of two of their members trying to get ahead. And they were upset with James and John because each of them wanted to push ahead—again out of some confused ideas of love and closeness for Jesus. Jesus sits them all down and tells them plainly that his love for his Father and for all of them is not aimed at privilege or getting ahead. Just the opposite. His love is a love totally poured out. It will always include a crucifixion, which is now not just a mark of a criminal's execution, but a symbol of a love poured out. His way of serving is to share all that he has—a sharing in his relationship with God, a sharing in his own divine life, a sharing in his Spirit and in his way of loving. Our way of serving, then, in order to be like Jesus' way, is the way of sharing. A life lived as a love poured out.

The second gospel passage for our prayer is John 20:11-18, the incident where Mary Magdalen meets up with the risen Jesus in the garden. Mary Magdalen is truly a woman in love. She loves Jesus and her grief at his death is inconsolable. Extraordinary things like an angel speaking to her from within the tomb seem to make no impression. When she is asked about her grieving, she presumes that this must be the one who keeps the cemetery garden. Without even looking up from her tears, she exclaims, "If you have his body, let me take it away." We might want to ask Mary how does she think that she can carry this dead body away. Who would she get to help her? But when she finally hears that voice say her name, she goes from sorrow to joy instantaneously. And she is holding Jesus tight so that he can never leave her again. Jesus calms her down in her exuberant joy. He indicates that his closeness to her is all part of her mission to share his presence with others. She must let go of her clinging in order that she can share his loving presence. Mary Magdalen is known as the apostle to the apostles. She shares what she has been given by the risen Lord. She serves by sharing. In our prayer, let Mary Magdalen share with us.

In order to deepen our own appreciation for sharing being a necessary part of our way of serving, I am proposing for our prayer Mark 10:35-45 and John 20:11-18. Let Ignatian contemplation enter you into the gospel and let repetition deepen your insight and affect and make it your own.

The grace that we pray for is: the grace to be generous in sharing what God has given us, both with God and with all those God brings into our lives.

Our mantra: "Lord, teach me to be generous. Teach me to serve you as you deserve."

To Serve Is Sharing

Points:

1. Our desire to share, our willingness to share, is a way of our serving.
2. A sharing out of love has no limits and it costs.
3. In sharing we never give away what we have; we only share.

Prayer Texts:

1. Mark 10:35-45, James and John request closeness to Jesus

2. John 20:11-18, Mary Magdalen and the risen Jesus

Mantra:

Lord, teach me to be generous.
Teach me to serve you as you deserve.

Prayer:

Ever bountiful God, you lavish your gifts upon us. Even more, you so identify yourself with us that Jesus is your Son enfleshed in our human family. Yet even while taking on our human nature forever in his risen life, Jesus promised us a second Paraclete, a Gift of your life always within us. You share with us your Spirit, the love bond of your Trinitarian Being. Love poured out is your way of serving us. Grant us the grace to respond to your love by our own life of sharing. May your Spirit strengthen us in our desire to live a life that is signalized by a love poured out.

We ask this in Jesus' name. Amen.

In Everything to Love and to Serve

Prayer

Loving God, your love streams out upon us like the rays of light from the sun that lightens and warms our whole earth. With Ignatius, we thank you for the never-ending flow of your love for us that is like the spring whose waters pour forth without limit. May your love empower us to love you ever more faithfully. Help us to live that love for you and for all our brothers and sisters in all the ways that your grace has allowed us to see and to appreciate as service. Grant that by your grace we may love and serve you in all things.

We ask this in Jesus' name. Amen.

In Everything to Love and to Serve

In the last prayer exercise titled "The Contemplation on the Love of God" in the Spiritual Exercises, Ignatius would have us ask for a grace that in everything we might love and serve the Lord. I believe that the positioning of the two words—first *amar* "to love" and then *servir* "to serve"—is important. Out of our love we are empowered to serve.

Often we have been inclined to limit service to the things we do, tasks to be performed. In our retreat we have been letting the gospels help lead us into a richer and more inclusive sense of serving. On this last day of retreat, I would like to return our focus more to the foundation of service—now, this last day of our retreat, not focusing on God's love as we did on the first day, but on our love response.

A most important moment in Ignatius's life happens when he is discouraged and confused about service. He had always been fired up by the idea of serving the Lord in the Holy Land. He had stirred the hearts of all his first companions with the same mission ideal. It is true that they had a second plan: to place themselves at the service of the pope for their mission, to be available for his sending. After a year of trying to get to the Holy Land and being closed out, Ignatius and his companions set out for Rome to see about fulfilling this second-best plan.

At a little town called La Storta, with its shrine chapel of Our Lady, Ignatius has an extraordinary mystical experience. He had been praying, like a mantra, that Our

61

Lady would place him with her Son. Feeling defeated in his ideal of serving God—a "working with" Jesus—in the Holy Land, Ignatius seems to want assurance of his "being with" Jesus. So Ignatius was imploring Mary to help him to gain a new and deeper intimacy—a renewed "being with"—Jesus. Then, maybe, he would be the more ready to "work with" Jesus, whatever service Jesus may indicate. *That* is the essence of his prayer to Mary, "Place me with your Son." The response to his prayer is beyond his imaginings.

Mary does not appear in his vision. We can believe only that this response from God is through her intercession. What Ignatius sees is God the Father, and Jesus carrying his cross. The Father says to Ignatius that "We will be propitious to you at Rome." And with that, the Father looks at Jesus and says, "I want you to take this man to serve us." Jesus, carrying his cross, says to Ignatius, "We want you to serve us."

Jesus' use of the word *you* is plural as reported in this vision. For Jesuits, the plural *you* has always meant that the grace or charism special to Ignatius is shared with all in the Society of Jesus. Today we would not hesitate to say that the grace or charism of Ignatius is shared with all those who find life in Ignatian spirituality. Jesus, on behalf of the Trinitarian God, is saying to each of us, "We want you to serve us."

Jesus carrying his cross is also a significant element. Jesus is not *on* the cross. Jesus is in action—*carrying* the cross, the ultimate symbol for us Catholics of a divine love poured out. Ignatian spirituality is forever branded by this vision. Love in service.

For our first prayer period, we might take the gospel passage, Matthew 11:25-30. This passage would have us listen in to Jesus' praying. Perhaps we can image the context of Jesus' prayer in relation to the return of the

62

disciples from a successful apostolic mission. It is their excitement and jubilation that elicits Jesus' prayer of thanks to his Father. We find this kind of context in Luke 10: 1-24. You might want to refer to this passage as you enter your prayer time.

Jesus is grateful and delights in the way his followers, whatever their talents are, are so graced by God that their ability to preach, teach, and work on behalf of the Kingdom of God is the glorification of God. God shines out and is manifest in their ways of serving. When Jesus reflects that he is the one who sent them out on mission, he again praises his Father for giving everything over to him. In the life of the Trinity, the Father serves the Son by sharing everything with him. Jesus, incarnate Son of God, serves the Father by sharing everything with him and by sharing everything of his grace and power with his followers.

Then Jesus addresses us, his followers about our service. In the midst of life's burdens and troubles, Jesus invites us to find rest and refreshment in our relationship with him. He uses a wonderfully dramatic image for how we will find his support. He describes his presence with us in terms of being yoked.

We are familiar with the yoke as the instrument that allows two animals, usually oxen, to pull together in plowing a field. Jesus, son of a carpenter, may well have made a number of yokes before he began his public life. He knew how to smooth a yoke so that it did not chafe the animals' necks as they pulled the plow or wagon. Jesus talks of sharing his yoke with us when he says "take my yoke upon your shoulders." We know then that Jesus desires that we be yoked with him. This desire for closeness with us is Jesus' reaching out to us in love. That makes the yoke easy, Jesus tells us, and working with Jesus makes all life's burdens light. Jesus serves us by sharing with us *his* yoke.

63

We share Jesus' mission by our being yoked with him. Being yoked with him is the mark of our service. Love follows upon love.

For our second prayer period, I would like us to return to the Ignatian exercise of the Contemplation on the Love of God. Commentators have interpreted the four points of the prayer exercises as a kind of review of the four Weeks of the Exercises. In the context of our retreat, I would have us focus the points by drinking in all the ways that God's love is shown in the ways that God is serving us. We remember that love is shown more in deeds than in words. But we also remember that the deeds "communicate" or talk.

As we review the many ways that God shows his love for us, we hear God saying to us that the ways of serving are many. To serve cannot be restricted to tasks performed or jobs done. "To serve," issuing from "to love," is a far richer and more subtle concept. Our prayer over these days has led us to appreciate all the ways that we can love God and express our love in the ways that we serve. To serve is rich in expression. Let us review in our prayer the consolations of this retreat time and be grateful.

In our first prayer period, I propose that we enter into our prayer from Matthew 11:25-30. In the second period of prayer, I suggest that we take up the Ignatian exercise on the Contemplation on the Love of God found in [230] – [237]. We are reviewing our love-responses to God and God's consolations experienced by us during this retreat time.

We remember that the grace we pray for is "in all things to love and to serve God our Lord."

Our mantra: "Lord, teach me to be generous. Teach me to serve you as you deserve."

Eighth Day

In Everything to Love and to Serve

Points:

1. "To serve" is rooted in and flows from our "to love."
2. Being yoked with Jesus makes the burdens of service light.
3. We serve Jesus carrying his cross.

Prayer Texts:

1. Matthew 11:25-30, we listen to Jesus' prayer and his promise
2. Contemplation on the Love of God, Sp Ex [230]-[237]

Mantra:

Lord, teach me to be generous.
Teach me to serve you as you deserve.

Prayer:

Loving God, your love streams out upon us like rays of light from the sun that lights and warms our whole earth. With Ignatius, we thank you for the never-ending flow of your love for us that is like the spring whose waters pour forth without limit. May your love empower us to love you ever more faithfully. Help us to live that love for you and for all our brothers and sisters in all the ways that your grace has allowed us to see and appreciate as service. Grant that by your grace we may love and serve you in all things.
We ask this in Jesus' name. Amen.

An Ignatian Retreat for People Somewhere on the Way

Contemplation on the Love of God

(somewhat abbreviated)

Preliminary Note: Before this exercise is presented, two observations should be made:

(1) the first is that love ought to show itself in deeds over and above words:

(2) the second is that love consists in a mutual sharing of goods. For example, as a lover one gives and shares with the beloved something of one's own personal gifts or some possession which one has or is able to give; so, too, the beloved shares in a similar way with the lover. In this way, one who has the knowledge shares it with the one who does not, and this is true for honors, riches, and so on. In love, one always want to give to the other.

The Setting: There are four different focal points which provide the subject matter for my prayer.

1. *God's gifts to me.* God creates me out of love and desires nothing more than a return of love on my part. So much does God love me that even though I turn away and make little response, the Giver of all good gifts continues to be my Savior and Redeemer. . . .

If I were to respond as a reasonable person, what could I give in return to such a Lover? Moved by love, I may want to express my own love-response in the following words:

Take and Receive

Take, Lord, and receive all my liberty, my memory, my understanding, and my entire will—all that I have and call my own. You have given it all to me. To you, Lord, I return it. Everything is yours; do with it what you will. Give me only your love and your grace. That is enough for me.

2. *God's self-giving to me.* God not only gives gifts to me, but literally gifts me with the fullness of divine life in Jesus. God's only Son is not only the Word in whom all things are created, but also the Word who becomes flesh and dwells with us. Jesus gives himself to me so that his body and blood become the food and drink of my life. Jesus pours out upon me his Spirit so that I can cry out "Abba, Father". . . .

If I were to make only a reasonable response, what could I do? Moved by love, I may find that I can respond best in words like the Take and Receive.

3. *God's labors for me.* God loves me so much, even entering into the very struggle of life. Like a potter with clay, like a mother in childbirth, or like a mighty force blowing life into dead bones, God labors to share divine life and love. God's labors are writ large in Jesus's passion and death on a cross in order to bring forth the life of the Resurrection.

Once more I question myself how I can make a response. Let me look again to the expression of the Take and Receive.

4. *God's unceasing giving and gifting.* God's love shines down upon me like the light rays from the sun, or God's love is poured forth lavishly like a fountain spilling forth its waters into an unending stream. Just as I see the sun in its rays and the fountain in its waters, so God pours forth a sharing in divine life in all the gifts showered upon me. . . .

What can I respond to such a generous Giver? Let me once again consider the expression of the Take and Receive.

Whatever is more conducive to the good closure of the retreat for the retreatant is the determining guide for how to proceed.

— from *Draw Me Into Your Friendship:*
A Contemporary Reading of the Exercises of St. Ignatius
by David L. Fleming SJ

67

Principle and Foundation

God who loves us creates us and wants to share life with us forever. Our loving response takes shape in our praise and honor and service of the God of our life.

All the things in this world are also created because of God's love and they are the gifts presented to us so that we can know God more easily and make a return of love more readily.

As a result, we show reverence for all the gifts of creation and collaborate with God in using them, so that by being good stewards we develop as loving persons in our care for God's world and its development. But if we misuse any of these gifts of creation or, on the contrary, make them the center of our lives, we break our relationship with God and hinder our growth as loving persons.

In everyday life, then, we must hold ourselves in balance before all created gifts, insofar as we have a choice and are not bound by some responsibility. We should not fix our desires on health or sickness, wealth or poverty, success or failure, a long life or a short one. For everything has the potential of calling forth in us a more loving response to our life forever with God.

Our only desire and our one choice should be this:

I want and I choose what better leads to God's deepening life in me.

— from *Draw Me Into Your Friendship:*
A Contemporary Reading of the Exercises of St. Ignatius
by David L. Fleming SJ

Appendix Two

Retreat Resources by the same author:

Draw Me Into Your Friendship: A Literal Translation and a Contemporary Reading of the Spiritual Exercises. St. Louis: Institute of Jesuit Sources, 1996.

Like the Lightning: The Dynamics of the Spiritual Exercises. St. Louis: Institute of Jesuit Sources, 2004.

Lessons from Ignatius Loyola. St. Louis: Review for Religious, 2005.

Discipleship and Its Foundations: A Jesuit Retreat. St. Louis: Review for Religious, 2005.

An Ignatian Retreat for People Somewhere on the Way

"We want you to serve us."

–St. Ignatius's vision at La Storta

Acknowledgment

For special contributions to the production of this book, I want to thank Mary Ann Foppe for preparing the text and overseeing its production, Tracy Gramm for the layout and design, and Michael Harter SJ for the photo of the Ignatian medallion on the cover, for the photo of the Holy Land carving of Christ carrying the cross on page 4 and for the photo of the Haitian carving of Christ carrying the cross on page 70. The seals and logos of the Society of Jesus used throughout the text are also the work of Michael Harter SJ.